Mama Rex & T

The
Reading Champion

by **Rachel Vail**

Illustrated by **Steve Björkman**

Scholastic Reader — Level 3

SCHOLASTIC INC. **Cartwheel B·O·O·K·S** ®

New York   Toronto   London   Auckland   Sydney
Mexico City   New Delhi   Hong Kong   Buenos Aires

For Liza and Aimee,
who are both absolute champions.
—R.V.

For Alex Uhl, who helps kids read.
—S.B.

ISBN 0-439-57822-1

Text copyright © 2003 by Rachel Vail.
Illustrations copyright © 2003 by Steve Björkman.
All rights reserved. Published by Orchard Books, an imprint of Scholastic Inc.
ORCHARD BOOKS and design are registered trademarks of
Watts Publishing Group, Ltd., used under license.
SCHOLASTIC and associated logos are trademarks and/or
registered trademarks of Scholastic Inc.

Library of Congress-in-Publication Data available.

10 9 8 7 6 5 4 3 2 1   04 05 06 07 08

Printed in the U.S.A. • First Scholastic Reader edition, March 2004

Contents

· ·

Chapter 1
A Jumble of Letters

T sat with Mrs. Sudak.
"You can do it, T," said Mrs. Sudak.
T looked at the page.

CRASH!

In the block corner, a castle fell.

T's best friend Walter stomped his foot.

"Bleh!" said Walter. "T, look!"

T and Walter had spent all morning building that castle.

Now it was ruined.

Mrs. Sudak pointed at the page. "What does this say, T?"

"I don't know," said T.

It just looked like a jumble of letters.

"Look at the word," said Mrs. Sudak.

T looked.

"Pickle?" T guessed.

"No," said Mrs. Sudak.

T guessed again. "Dragon?"

T looked out the window.

He wanted to be under the tree.

Mrs. Sudak pointed at the book. "This word here."

"Cake? Dog? Book?"

"Um," said Mrs. Sudak.

"See?" said T. "It doesn't help to look."

T put his head down.

"Can I go to blocks?" he asked.

Mrs. Sudak said, "I will give you my secret trick."
T looked up.
"It is called Magic Boxes," said Mrs. Sudak.
"You are good at clues. Right, T?"
T nodded, a little.
He and Walter played Deep Detectives
almost every day.

"Look!" Mrs. Sudak yelled.

T looked.

"A clue is in the Magic Box!" said Mrs. Sudak. The magic box was just Mrs. Sudak's fingers. They covered up almost the whole page, all but one letter.

"That is not a clue," said T. "That is an F."

"Aha!" said Mrs. Sudak. "And what sound does an F make?"

T made the F sound. Then he looked at the block corner.

Walter was reading a big, thick book.

Walter was a reading champion.

T slumped down in his chair.

"Another clue," said Mrs. Sudak.

"This is a hard one."

T glanced down.

"It is an A," he said.

"What is so hard about that?"

"Hmm," said Mrs. Sudak.

She moved the Magic Box until another letter appeared.

He smiled. "That is my favorite," he said. "T."

"Now put the sounds together," said Mrs. Sudak.

"Then can I go to blocks?" asked T.

Mrs. Sudak nodded, so T tried.

"Ffff –aaaa – T. Fffff-aaaa-t. Fat. Fat. Fat."

"Well, I've been trying to eat fewer donuts," said Mrs. Sudak.

T smiled. "I read 'fat'?"

"You put the clues together. You figured it out," said Mrs. Sudak.

"Yes," said T. "I did."

"You may go to blocks now."

"Great." T stood up to go. "Mrs. Sudak? How many words are there?"

"In the world?" asked Mrs. Sudak. "I don't know. Thousands and thousands."

"Oh," said T. "And I can read a grand total of one of them."

Sadly, he walked away, toward the blocks.

Chapter 2
Stinky and Great

After school, Mama Rex asked, "What did
you learn today?"
"I learned to read," said T.
"Really?" asked Mama Rex.
"Yes," said T. "I can read the word FAT."
"Oh," said Mama Rex. "OK."
"Let me know if you need me to read it,"
said T. "Any time."

Mama Rex and T walked along for a while.
"I have to get my nails done," Mama Rex said.
"Yuck," said T. "The nail place is stinky."
They looked in the window of a bookstore.
"I will buy you a book," said Mama Rex. "You
can read while we are there."
"OK," said T. "But it will have to be a book
with the word FAT in it."

Mama Rex and T went into the bookstore.
"Hello," said Mama Rex to the man behind
the counter.
"Do you have a good book for a young
dinosaur who can read the word FAT?"
The man scratched his chin.
He looked up.
T looked up.
Nothing was there.
"Yes," said the man. He walked away.

Mama Rex and T waited.

Soon, the man was back with a book.

He gave the book to T.

"FAT!" yelled T. He pointed at the word he knew how to read.

"We will take it," said Mama Rex.

T carried the book to the nail place.

"See?" T said to Mama Rex. "Stinky."

"Yes," said Mama Rex. "Very stinky."

T sat next to Mama Rex's foot. He opened his new book.

There was a word after FAT.

T looked at each letter, one at a time. C–A–T. *CAT*, read T. *FAT CAT*.

T smiled. It was a good book.

T opened the book.
There were a lot of letters on the page.
T tried to get his fingers to make a magic box.
It didn't work as well as Mrs. Sudak's,
but he kept trying.

P–A–T, read T. *PAT.*
PAT SAT.
PAT SAT ON A FAT CAT.
SPLAT!

T laughed.

"Are you having fun?" asked Mama Rex.

"Yes," said T. He kept going.

DRAT! SAID PAT.
A FLAT CAT!

T laughed so hard he bumped into the table.

Mama Rex bent down. "What are you doing?"

T tried to catch his breath. "Pat!"

"Pat?" asked Mama Rex.

"Pat splatted the cat!" said T.

He turned the page.

"Listen," he said. He slowly read out loud:

I AM A CAT, YELLED THE FLAT FAT CAT.
NOT A MAT!

T laughed so hard he fell down.

"T," said Mama Rex. "I think..."
T stopped laughing. "What?"
"I think you know how to read," she said.

T looked back at his book.
Nobody had read the story to him.
He had read it himself.
The letters had become — words.

T nodded. "I can read."
"Hooray for you!" Mama Rex shouted.
She twirled T around and around.
Her nail polish was ruined, but she didn't
even care.
"I can read!" T yelled. "I am a Reading
Champion!"

Chapter 3
Sweet Dreams

Mama Rex tucked T into bed.

"Have sweet dreams," said Mama Rex.

"I will," said T.

"Ouch," said Mama Rex.

She reached under the blanket.

A book.

She smiled and pulled it out.

Mama Rex tried to tuck T in again.

"Sweet dreams...ouch!"

She pulled out another book.

She tucked him in a third time.

"Sweet — ouch!" she yelled.

Mama Rex picked up T's blanket.

She looked under.

She saw T.

And she saw all his books.

"T!" said Mama Rex.

T smiled. "I wish the whole world were made of books."

"Your whole bed is," said Mama Rex. "How are you going to sleep?"

"I don't think I can," said T. "I'm too happy. I want to read every book in the world."

Mama Rex smiled back at T.

"I know the feeling," she said. "But you can't do it all tonight."

"Aw," moaned T.

Mama Rex made space between the stacks
of books.

She sat on the bed next to T.

"But," she said, "you can start."

T grinned. "Do you want me to read to you?"

"Yes," said Mama Rex. "I do."

"I'm not great at it yet," said T. "I may need
some help."

"That's why I'm here," said Mama Rex.

It was past T's bedtime.
Mama Rex and T didn't notice.
They were reading.